From Monkey, Man to God and The Different Degrees of Monkeyism

J. Lazarus Muyet

Old New York LLC

Also By J. Lazarus Muyet

The Hidden History of the Gods and the Subjugation of Humanity

Orishas Worship and the Sixteen Truths of IFA

Universal Laws

Quotes From Behind Bars

To my brother and comrade in the struggle, Gregory Milton, for giving me the idea of the different degree of Monkeyism.

"Most people are other people. Their thoughts are someone else's opinion; their lives are a mimicry".

-Oscar Wilde

Contents

Preface   2

Introduction   13

1. The First-Degree of Monkeyism   17
   (The Subterranean Monkey)

2. The Second-Degree of Monkeyism   29
   (The Manufactured Monkey)

3. The Third-Degree Monkey   41
   (The Intelligent Monkey)

4. The Stage of Man   48

5. Reality Shifter   58

6. The State of God   64

"Men fear thought as they fear nothing else on earth, more than ruin, more than death. Thought is subversive and revolutionary, destructive and terrible, thought is merciless to privilege, established institutions, and comfortable habit. Thought looks into the pit of hell and is not afraid. Thought is great and swift and free, the light of the world, and the chief glory of man".
                              -Bertrand Russell, Philosopher

Preface

I like to think of myself as a sociologist. Though I do not possess a bachelor's degree in sociology, I have spent close to three decades in the Federal Bureau of Prisons, intensively studying human behavior. I like to believe that this qualifies me, at least to a degree, as being an expert on behavioral science.

Though my observation of how an individual acts within a social setting is limited to penal institutions, prisons are actually micro reflections of macro-societies. In fact, a prison Chaplin once told me that when the government wants to implement a new law(s) in society, they first experiment within the prisons five years prior to them actually implementing them in the 'Free World' as most prisoners refer to it.

There are two reasons for this: The first reason is that prisoners are believed to be the most aggressive, and those with long sentences usually have nothing to lose. So, when prison officials implement a new rule and the prison population passively accepts it without any kind of resistance, then the government knows that they can easily implement this same rule -or a similar law- in society where people do have a lot to lose.

The second reason is that prison is a small controlled area where subjects can easily be observed. Staff can watch the body language of how one reacts to a rule that strips away more of the prisoners' privileges. Those who exhibit any willingness to oppose this new rule, either through physical aggression or intellectual defiance, are quickly identified and then isolated from the rest of the population. In society, the government uses this same tactic to identify and create 'files' on those who speak out and protest against them. These dissenters are labeled 'terrorist' and 'criminals' through mass media propaganda, solely because they choose not to conform to the ways of the establishments.

Prison is the lowest level of existence, and being trapped in a small confined area for a long period of time brings out the true character of a person. I have seen inmates act in ways that are abnormal, but which they perceive to be 'normal' because others around them are doing it.

Most prisoners are automatons, doing the same thing every day without ever questioning why. Every morning when the cells crack open the same prisoners put their chairs in the same spot, in front of the same television, watching the same programs every single day. There is no variation, no change in their uninterrupted tedious schedule. This is because the vast majority of them have no actual purpose for their existence. They spend their days watching television, working out, playing cards, dominoes, chess, and playing and watching sports to occupy their time. Only a handful of them actually utilize their time rising above their deteriorating conditions by educating themselves.

There is not much of a difference between those who are physically imprisoned and those in society who mistakenly believe that they are 'free'; they are both spiritually and mentally immured in some 'reality' that fully occupies their time. The vast majority of people in the 'free world' live out their entire existence on autopilot. They wake up in the morning and eat breakfast; go to work, come home and eat dinner, watch television and then go to bed, only to repeat this monotonous routine the following day. Usually there is only small variations in their daily lives.

As I already mentioned, prison is a micro reflection of a macro society. Of course, society is separated into different classes so when I say 'society;' I am basically referring to the poor income areas whose inhabitants make up the majority of the prison population. Distinction of race makes no difference because contrary to popular belief, there are all nationalities -including 'whites'- residing in these poor communities. These places are referred to as ghettos and trailer parks. What they are called makes no difference. What they are is small enclosed areas -like prisons- that keep their inhabitants economically and socially trapped inside, while making them feels as if they belong there. This is why most prisoners are content with being incarcerated; it's a reflection of their 'reality'. While those who live in Suburbia America view incarceration as a stigma, for those who are born and raised in these low-income areas -especially among the criminal element- in their twisted and perverted thinking, a stint in prison is a badge of honor, a rite of passage.

Prison does one or two things to a man: It either makes him psychologically and spiritually stronger or it breaks him down completely until he is nothing more than a shell of his old self. I once read somewhere that in time of great uncertainty, people will either behave with great strength or weakness, and very little in-between. Most succumb to the latter. "A weak character is a defect that, under critical circumstances, certainly leads to disastrous consequences; there is a void that nothing can fill."[1]

The degrees of their weakness (or what I refer to as 'mental defect'), varies, according to each individual, and many, if not most, need a

---

1. Jaime Balmes

crutch to lean on to help carry them through the onslaught of raw realities they have come face to face with.

Prison, like those poor income areas whose inhabitant are mentally and economically trapped inside, effect people differently. Many unconsciously accept their environment and lose their individuality by joining an organization, i.e., a religion, a gang, or a group of 'homies' that homogeneously lumps them together, erasing all traces of their individual self. "The loss of self has increased the necessity to conform, for it results in a profound doubt of ones identity."[2]

I have observed how these types of people come into prison afraid, not only of the environment but the mere thought of being alone, so they gravitate to whatever group they feel can save them from the pain of loneliness. Many of them suddenly find 'God', as if this omnipotent and omnipresent being has somehow been hiding, and for some odd reason prison seems to be the only place where a person can find Him.

Some become Muslims, metamorphosizing into the prototype of what a Muslim is supposed to look like: Growing big beards; forced to give up pork; wearing the leg cuffs of their pants rolled up as if they are travelling in the desert; praying five times a day; greeting each other with As-salamu alaykum, and now want to be referred to by their 'Arabic name'. Every single one of them looking identical to the other.

There was a time when Muslims in prison were the embodiment of militancy and revolutionary consciousness. They, like so many other prisoners of the past who felt the yoke of oppression tangled around their neck, stood up against the injustice and abuse by sadistic prison guards. But now they have evolved -or better yet devolved- especially the Sunni Muslims, into nothing more than an organization that

---

2. Erich Fromm, Escape from Freedom

harbors and protects snitches; men who have betrayed and sold their families and friends into slavery, for the proverbial price of 30 pieces of silver in the guise of time reduction.

Others become 'Christians', but instead of Allah it's Jesus who's their Lord and Savior. They walk around with Bibles tightly clenched in their hands and their 'holier than thou' attitudes, arguing that their truth is the only truth, and according to them, will be the only ones allowed to enter the Pearly Gates of Heaven.

Ironically though, most of these so-called 'Christians' are usually pedophiles and rapist who aren't seeking repentance for the abhorrent acts they committed against women and children. They become 'Christians' solely because it's the only group -besides the Sunni Muslims- who will openly embrace them wholeheartedly because they share a common illness.

This has become the accepted norm within these two 'religious' groups; men who have compromised their moral and ethical principles by embracing snitches and sexual deviants -the bottom feeders of humanity even within the prison pecking order- simply because they 'worship' the same 'gods.' This hypocrisy is so deeply embedded into the collective psyche of the prison population, that in prison today, men who are 'stand-up', meaning not a rat or sexual deviant, but is in fact, a person of good character even though he's judged differently by conservative Americans in society, are the ones who are ostracized in this newly created Bizarro World. And everyone gladly accepts this new norm without ever questioning how it became like this.

For those who religion doesn't appeal to, the next best thing is to get initiated into a gang that has been spreading cancerously within and outside the prison. But now that they are part of a gang and forfeited their right to individual thought, they are no longer able to walk anywhere by themselves, and instead, are forced to walk as a unit

– One Body, One Mind. They must stand guard as their 'brothers' take showers and use the bathroom, or when ordered must beat, stab, or even kill someone on command of their leader.

During the 60's ,70's and early 80's when teenagers who were in a gang or a crew usually gave up their affiliation when they reached the age of 18; the age Policy Makers labels an individual an adult in which he must begin taking responsibility for his actions. (Except of course if you are black or Latino and committed a crime, then, as young as 14 you can be charged as an adult, especially if the victim is white). But within the last two decades there has been a considerable rise in the age difference of gang members. Now there are guys in their 30's, 40's 50's, and some even in their 60's who are still 'gangbanging', 'throwing-up' gang signs, and taking orders from 'leaders' half their ages.

The Heavyweight Champion Muhammed Ali once said something to the effect, that if you are doing the same thing when you are fifty that you were doing when you were twenty, then you really haven't grown. What's really shocking is that some of these 'diehard' gang members joined when they were already in their late 30's and 40's; showing that they have no actual purpose for their existence. "Until thought is linked with purpose there is no intelligent accomplishment."[3]

Then you have those who get on 'Homey-Time.' To explain what I mean by that I must first point out that the Federal Bureau of Prisons are the most racially diversified places in America. Everyone is categorized into race and gangs, and you are labeled a gang member regardless of whether or not you are actually in one. Those who are not members of a gang refer to themselves as being 'Independent' or 'Neutral' but this is a misnomer. Since the Federal Bureau of Prisons, unlike State Correctional Facilities, ship their prisoners ("property")

---

3. James Allen, As A Man Thinkith

all across the United States and this, for the most part, forces those who come from the same state or geographical area to flock together. Those who come from the same state often refer to each other as 'homeys' and use the jargon 'car' to mean what group they belong to.

An example of this behavior goes like this: When an individual enters a prison the other prisoners automatically question him, wanting to know "with who he runs with?" If he is neutral and let's say, from New York; his response would be that he "runs with New York." The further away you are from your state, the more alliances are made. These same 'homeys' from New York now 'run' with New Jersey, Connecticut, and in some prisons, Boston. Now, this group of 'homeys' just got larger. So therefore, in actuality, these 'cars' are nothing more than gangs.

While there are a few people in the group who don't necessarily share the 'group mentality;' those people tend to suppress their thoughts. Because in certain environments to think and act differently from the aggregated group is to court danger. Plus, a man who tries to stand alone is isolated and left to fend for himself.

The type of people I have described above have given up their individuality; the freedom of being able to think for themselves in exchange for being part of a collective group. This makes them feel as if they have a place where they belong.

> "If everyone is thinking alike then someone isn't thinking."[4]

Then you have those who refuse to assimilate; refuse to conform to the norm of what is happening around them; and struggle to

---

4. George S. Patton, Military Commander

overcome the obstacles in their way. These people are unique in a world where everyone thinks, acts, and looks alike.

In this pamphlet I have made an attempt to define what Monkeyism is, and categorized the degree a person belongs to according to their level of awareness and intelligence. There are some people who might feel offended by the word "Monkey" because of its derogatory connotation, and how it has been applied as a racial epithet towards a particular race. But Monkey in this context is applied symbolically to people of all races. The word Man symbolizes the both sexes, and 'God' signifies an individual who possesses a profound spiritual understanding.

Monkeyism is divided into three distinctly different degrees, because though the masses possess an innate mechanism to mimic one another, they also possess different level of intelligence. Therefore, I have separated people's mind state, and thus their social behavior into the First, Second, and Third Degree of Monkeyism. I have also attempted to define the Stage of Man as well as the State of God. Each of these degrees of mental evolution is easily recognizable by a person's action.

The allegorical story below written by an unknown writer, is the perfect symbolic story of how the masses have accepted their condition without ever questioning it. Whether the actual experiment was ever performed, or the author invented it through his own observation of human behavior is irrelevant. What is relevant is that humanity, on different levels, are conditioned through a variety of different programs, which systematically brainwashes them to think and act a certain way without ever putting any thought into questioning them.

- Start with a cage containing five monkeys.

- Inside the cage, hang a banana on a string and place a set of stairs under it.

- Before long, a monkey will go to the stairs and start to climb towards the banana.

- As soon as he touches the stairs, spray all the monkeys with cold water.

- After a while, another monkey makes an attempt with the same result all the monkeys are sprayed with cold water.

- Pretty soon when a monkey tries to climb the stairs, the other monkeys will try to prevent it.

- Now put away the cold water.

- Remove one monkey from the cage and replace it with a new one.

- The new monkey sees the banana and wants to climb the stairs, [but] to his surprise and horror, all of the monkeys attack him.

- After another attempt and attack, he knows that if he tries to climb the stairs, he will be assaulted,

- Next, remove another original monkey and replace it with a new one. The newcomer goes to the stairs and is attacked.

- The previous newcomer takes part in the punishment with enthusiasm! Likewise, replace a third original monkey with a new one, then a fourth, then a fifth.

- Every time the newest monkey takes to the stairs, he is attacked. Most of the monkeys that are beating him have no idea why they are not permitted to climb the stairs, or why they are participating in the beating of the newest monkey.

- After replacing all the original monkeys, none of the remaining monkeys have ever been sprayed with cold water.

- Nevertheless, no monkey ever again approaches the stairs to try for the banana.

- Why not? Because as far as they know that's the way it's always been.

Free thinkers are those who are willing to use their minds without prejudice and without fearing to understand things that clash with their own customs, privileges, or beliefs. This state of mind is not common, but it is essential for right thinking; where it is absent, discussion is apt to become worse than useless."

-Leo Tolstoy, author

Introduction

It is a known fact that each individual perceives God according to his or her own level of comprehension, and therefore the more conscious a man is -both intellectually and spiritually- the more profound his understanding of God becomes. I personally think that too many people are disillusioned with the concept of what God is. But I blame that on the fact that the majority of the human race does not possess the inquisitive nature, nor the desire and the determination to search deep within themselves to find out who they truly are.

If a man who is mentally and spiritually illuminated defines himself as a god, and claims that through the secret teachings he is able to uplift and transform a man from a savage to a civilize state and then into a perfect being, he will be ostracized, imprisoned, and even murdered for claiming to be something other than what the masses want him to be.

The reason for this is because man, regardless of how advance he thinks he is among the animal kingdom, is still in the lowest state of evolution; a primate, or as I often refer to them as, Monkeys. When I use the term "Monkey", it isn't being used in the same sense as Darwin's theory that man evolved or sprang from a family of primates. And though it has been scientifically proven that we share a large percentage of our DNA with those of a primate, here I am not speaking of an anthropoid or corporeal evolution but a mental and spiritual one.

My usage of the term "Monkey", "Man", and "God" is metaphorical symbolizing a man's growth from a savage to a civilized state to a perfect being. Monkeyism refers not only to a person's mental state, but as well as their despondent need to mimic others around them. Therefore, I have coined the word "Monkeyism" to mean a psychological behavior pattern of imitating other people's vernacular, style of fashion, and demeanor solely because everyone around them is doing it.

Most people assimilate into this behavior pattern of mimicking others around them simply because they don't want to feel ostracized, and thus looked upon as being different from everyone else. This is done unconsciously through peer pressure. Usually, at a young age one is indoctrinated into a false belief system of conformity, that after years of acceptance it has cultivated into being part of their nature.

This is why most people from the same geographical area and same class -mainly the lower income and middle class- all look and act alike wearing the same footwear, the same designer clothes, and speak in the same vernacular; they have lost the identity of self. One writer once wrote: "You laugh at me because I'm different; I laugh at you because you're all the same."[1]   These people have given up their individuality and have become nothing more than a conglomeration of human bodies. The author Erich Fromm writes:

---

1. Anthony the Great

"The individual ceases to become himself; he adopts the kind of personality offered by cultural patterns, and therefore becomes exactly as others expect him to be... The person who gives up his individual self and becomes an automaton, identical with millions of other automatons around him, need not feel alone and anxious anymore. But the price he pays, however, is high, it is the loss of his self."[2]

The historian Manly P. Hall wrote that "all humans [are] divided into four general classes... the lowest of these divisions is physical nature, and those who dwell therein, they live only for [the] gratification of their physical nature."[3] Eighty-five percent of the masses; the symbolically deaf, dumb, and blind are Monkeys in one form or another. There are several types of Monkeys of different races, classes and degrees, but here again I am specifically speaking of an individual's mind state. Any person is a Monkey who is inherently weaker than the mental impulses about him. Most people are considered Monkeys because they are not self-determined, though they might falsely believe that they are. Therefore, I stress the fact that the word Monkey isn't being used in a derogatory term, or directed to any specific group of people, but applies to all different races and classes and the social behavior within their pseudo reality.

Man, in his lowest nature, is nothing more than an unevolved specie who has been conditioned to act irrationally and on impulse. An ancient philosopher is quoted as stating:

---

2. Escape From Freedom

3. What the Ancient Wisdom Expert of Its Disciples

"He who has knowledge of common things is a brute among men. He who has accurate knowledge of human concern alone is a man among brutes. But he who knows all that can be known by intellectual energy, is a god among men. Man's status in the natural world is determined by the quality of his thinking. He whose mind is enslaved by bestial instincts is philosophically not superior to the brute, he whose rational faculties ponder human affairs is a man; and he whose intellect is elevated to the consideration of divine realities is already a demigod..."[4]

Everyone, regardless of what degree they fall into -Monkey, Man, or even those who have reached the ne plus ultra state of God- share a collective mind state. Once the inception of consciousness (awareness) strips you of all illusions, it transcends your perception of reality to different levels. Yes, there are different levels of consciousness, and the higher your consciousness rises the more transparent your perception of 'reality' becomes. Then what happens is then you will be able to recognize the different degrees of Monkeyism.

---

4. The Secret Teachings of All Ages

Chapter 1

The First-Degree of Monkeyism

(The Subterranean Monkey)

"One tenth of humanity will have the right to individuality and will exercise unlimited authority over nine tenths. The latter will lose their individual[ity] and will become a flock of sheep; compelled to passive obedience. They will be led back to original innocence and so to speak, to the primitive paradise, where nevertheless, they must work."

-Boris Verkhovensky (The Possessed)

Ignorance is not a simple lack of knowledge but an aversion to knowledge, the refusal to know."

-Karl Popper

"According to the Mysteries, the monkey represents the condition of man before the rational soul entered into his constitution. Therefore, it typifies the irrational man. By some, the monkey is looked upon as a specie not ensouled by the spiritual hierarchies, by others as a fallen [spirit], wherein man has been deprived of his divine nature through degeneracy."

-Manly P. Hall (Historian and Freemason)

The First-Degree of Monkeyism -which compromises of the vast majority of the American population- I have coined Subterranean Monkeys. The reason being is that their intelligence and awareness is so deeply buried within them, that it is almost non-existent. Those who fall into this degree are those who are so mentally and spiritually dead, that they are not even conscious of a world that exist outside their mind. Everything they do is mechanical, and like a machine that has been pre-programmed to operate with limited functions, these Monkeys whose minds exist within the lower region of intelligence, also follow a predetermined sequence of operation. They live their day-to-day existence off their indoctrination; meaning that they think, speak and act according to certain influences within their environment.

For them life has no real purpose other than to breed and satisfy their primal animalistic nature. Their 'reality' is constructed by walls of materialism, but their desire for material things is simply limited to owning the latest fashion in footwear and designer clothes. Those who do acquire enough money to make a difference and change their destiny, would rather spend it on expensive cars and jewelry; that's the furthest that they are able to expand their dreams. Never do they think of investing their money into higher education, so that their off-springs in future generations will produce things of value. They are born and then they die, never realizing that life can be other than what it is.

Those in this degree are collectively viewed as a mindless mass of human flesh who succumb to every physical desire. They move aimlessly through life and for this reason are often referred to as Zombies, Sleepwalkers, and the Walking Dead. This is because they are nothing more than an empty shell of a body that has been deprived of its conscious powers and are therefore incapable of moral judgement. Socrates once wrote:

"The ignorant man is dead while still alive."

I often refer to this species as the Wasted Ones, because their mind is so deteriorated from lack of use, that they are basically "wasting" their life away. This is the lowest state of existence there is, (without actually being physically dead), and for many of them there is no hope of ever being awakened from psychological sleep state. P.D. Ouspensky writes of those who possess this mindset.

> "[The Subterranean] is not a completed being, [in that] nature develops him to a certain point and then leaves him either to develop further by his own efforts and devices, or to live and die such as he was born... [He] does not realize that he is actually a machine, with no independent movement which is brought into motion by external influences. The most important of the qualities which man ascribes to himself; but does not possess, is consciousness. By consciousness we mean a particular kind of awareness in man, awareness of who he is, what he feels or thinks, or where he is at the moment."[1]

The Subterranean is a blight of nature who is mentally and spiritually underdeveloped. While there are a few of these Monkeys who have risen above their deteriorating conditions by focusing their intellectual energy in attaining their goal, the vast majority of them are content in wallowing in a cesspool of ignorance and have accepted their fate. Many of those who fall into this degree are barbaric in their behavior and this makes them easily recognizable. They are loud, obnoxious, and inconsiderate towards others. The reason for this is

---

1. Conscience: The Search for Truth

because they are incapable of rationalizing and thus lack any degree of commonsense.[2]

One of the many ways of distinguishing a Subterranean is their continuous need to express themselves. They are constantly talking, and people who talk a lot usually don't have anything important to say. The reason that they are afraid of being quiet is because they are afraid of what their mind is trying to tell them. Many of these Monkeys are not able to hold a conversation in a civilized manner.

They have a tendency to always scream in an attempt to get their point across, even when the person with whom they are speaking with is standing directly in front of them. Their exhibitionistic nature compels them to yell and make unnecessary noise solely for the sake of performing for an audience because they crave attention. Of course, not all Subterraneans share these traits; there are some who are less boisterous and introverted but these are few in numbers.

Then you have those who suffer from the inability to dress properly. Within the past decade an epidemic of large proportion has affected the male specie, having them believe that it is 'cool' to wear their pants sagging, advertising to the people around them the crack of their buttock. There was time, especially inside the penal system, if a man wore his pants hung low showing off his buttocks, it was because he was a 'punk', a homosexual who was letting others know that he was either available or 'selling' himself for his pimp lover. Now, for some odd reason that is unexplainable, this has become the style, and of course these Monkeys see nothing wrong with this imbecilic and improper behavior, because their 'reality' dictates that this is the norm among a certain collective group of people. Homo sapiens are a herd-like specie, and those who share a collective mind state will always gravitate towards each other.

---

2. According to Merriam-Webster Collegiate Dictionary, common-sense means "sound and prudent judgement based on simple perception of the situation or facts.

Another recognizable sign of a Subterranean is their immaturity; their refusal to grow up. Sure, physically they are aging, but mentally and spiritually they are stuck in their adolescent years. The psychologist and author Na'im Akbar referred to it as being trapped in their "Baby Stage." Mass media is promoting a psychological death of grown-ups, which in turn is producing a nation of adults with childish mentalities.

I have observed "men" in their 40's and 50's having conversations with teenagers or those still in their 20's, and the only thing that comes out of their mouth is gibberish. Instead of their association being based on a teacher protégé relationship where the younger one is learning from the older one, it's based on nothing more than buffoonery. So instead of the younger generation looking at the older generation as one would look at an elder -with genuine respect- they look at them as equals. The old adage "with age comes maturity", isn't necessarily true. Manly P. Hall wrote:

> "The average man... has the eternal rational and emotional equipment approximating the standard of values of a twelve to fourteen year old child. This is his true age in the universe, even though he may be octogenarian in physical years. His notions and opinions may have the appearance of maturity, but his actions are impelled by his internal capacity to estimate the consequence of his own conduct. It is his conduct that reveals clearly his psychological immaturity."[3]

Since I am writing this while incarcerated, I must point out that prison was once viewed as a University of Higher Learning. Those who came to prison as social criminals usually left much more

---

3. Sages & Seers

educated than when they first arrived. Many of them became educators, self-help counselors, political activist, and some even turned revolutionaries and visionaries. Now, the only thing they care about is what drugs are being sold in the prison yard; what's the latest shows that they can lose themselves in, and what's the newest pair of sneakers being sold in commissary.

The fact is that those who fall into this degree are encumbered with such inferior intellect, that they are either completely illiterate or have very limited education, and therefore have no real desire to rise above their inferior status. They care only about nonessential and superficial things. Their everyday conversation pertains only to sports, pseudo 'Reality Shows' and music videos; things of no real importance. They know exactly how much money an entertainer is making; how many games a certain team has won, but yet they are unable to tell you about anything that has any real substance in their life. The heroes that they look up to aren't the men and women who have fought against oppression by sacrificing their lives for the greater good. No, their heroes are men who can shoot a basketball through a hoop, or who can run fast with a football in their hands. They look up to singers and rappers and fantasize their meaningless existence through the lives of entertainers. "The surest way to corrupt a youth is to instruct him to hold in higher esteem those who think alike than those who think differently."[4]

These individuals (as a collectiveness) are the ramification of America's attempt to dumb down its citizens. Never do they engage in stimulating conversation that pertains to spiritual and mental growth, or issues that are relevant to freeing themselves from psychological enslavement.

The Austrian neurologist and psychologist Sigmund Freud stated that *the masses never thirsted after the truth.* These people are

---

4. Friedrich Nietzsche, Philologist and philosopher

so mind manipulated by entertainment and propaganda, and thus enslaved into an illusional world, that many will never be able to free themselves from the box that they are contained within. And for many, freedom isn't even a yearning. Someone once wrote that "Happy slaves are the bitter enemies of freedom."[5] Ignorance is indeed bliss.

Since the majority of those in this degree have such a below average intelligence, they tend to function strictly on emotions and thus act on impulse and with an irrational behavior. Manly P. Hall writes:

> "When confronted with a problem involving the use of reasoning faculties, individuals of strong intellect keep their poise, and seek to reach a solution by obtaining facts bearing upon the question. Those of immature mentality, on the other hand, are overwhelmed. While the former may be qualified to solve the riddle of their destiny, the latter must be led like a flock of sheep and taught in simple language."[6]

Any attempt to try and help those in this degree is dangerous, because many of them suffer from an inferiority complex, and tend to act aggressively towards anyone they feel is more intelligent than they are. If you genuinely attempt to awaken them from their slumber they will attack you -either verbally or physically- believing in their mind that your efforts to assist them is really a mockery to highlight their mental capacity. The play writer and Nobel Prize winner George Bernard Shaw is said to have come to a profound understanding, that trying to help others is an exceedingly dangerous occupation.

---

5. Marie von Ebner-Eschenbach

6. The Secret Teachings of All Ages

These types of people must be left alone at all costs, especially once they have reached a certain age. It isn't because after a certain age one is not able to acquire new information. On the contrary. Man is a creature who possesses the unique ability to acquire, absorb, and retain new information at any age as long as he continuously utilizes his mind. The reason they say that "you can't teach an old dog new tricks" is because of their stubbornness to explore the terra incognita of their own mind. They are comfortable in the state that they are existing in and don't want anybody disturbing it.

Another sign that distinguishes these Monkeys is their constant need to complain and whine about their conditions, but yet will not make any serious attempts to change it. Not because they are not able to but because they choose not to, and instead, are constantly blaming others for their pitiful conditions that they find themselves in. "A man only begins to be a man when he ceases to whine and revile and commences to search for the hidden justice which regulates his life.[7]

It is these types of people who the Bible refers to as sheep. Because by refusing to change their thinking they have allowed others to manipulate their destiny while they wander around aimlessly. They look for others to lead them while they gladly follow without ever questioning. "Leaders think and talk about solutions, followers think and talk about problems."[8]

The truth is that no matter how much these Monkeys complain they are actually content with their conditions. Because a person who is truly frustrated with the predicament that they find themselves in, will do everything within their power to create a change. They rebel. Their rebelliousness doesn't necessarily have to be a physical one, it can be a mental and spiritual rebellion; they change their

---

7. James Allen, As a Man Thinketh

8. Brian Tracy, Author

thinking thus changing their conditions. A person who doesn't rebel has accepted the fact that he is imprisoned in a psychological enslavement, and so instead of trying to bend the bars of their imprisonment, they instead try to escape from freedom. José Ortega y Gasset writes:

> "The masses think that it is easy to flee from reality, when it is the most difficult thing in the world."

For them 'freedom' is keeping themselves occupied with mindless forms of entertainment: sports, television, gambling, partying, etc. Within the last few years pseudo 'Realty Shows' and talk shows have become the big craze on television. People broadcasting their lives in front of the cameras for the world to see, while millions of viewers are glued in front of the television set fixated on the lives of other people, instead of putting their own lives in order. They have become trapped in a virtual reality and are turning into a race of zombies.

Others find their 'escape' through alcohol/and or drugs - whether illicit or pharmaceutical, because for them it is much easier facing the world through a distorted perception; it gives them the illusion as if they are free. For those who don't want to be entertained, or walk through life in an alcohol or drug induced state, find their 'freedom' through the comfort of religion; the oldest and most powerful mind manipulation that ever existed. As one unknown writer wrote:

> "Religion is a delusion that the oppress indulge in to avoid being confronted with the harsh reality of their condition[s]. [It] holds out false promise of living a meaningful life now, to be followed by eternal bliss later. In doing so it keeps the masses complacent. The only

way the masses can escape the reality of the situation is
to break free."

The question that I have often asked myself numerous times
throughout my own mental and spiritual evolution, and my
observation of social behavior, is why do people continue to
complain but refuse to change? The answer I've discovered is simple.
They refuse to seek change because they are mentally and spiritually
weak. "It has been said that power corrupts. But it is perhaps equally
important to realize that weakness, too corrupts. Power corrupts the
few, while weakness corrupts the many."[9] They lack what I have
termed the Four Sacred D's: Desire, Determination, Discipline, and
Dedication. One must first have the desire to want to change. Then
they must have a strong determination that comes with discipline
and dedication.

C.D. Lawson writes:

> "The reason why those who are mentally weak remain
> in submission to inferior environment[s] is because they
> [do not] use their mental powers resisting adversity. "[10]

Those who fall into this degree do not possess any will of their own
and have no real desire to be anything other than what they are:
weaklings. They will always be slaves to their lower selves, and "a slave
loses everything in their chains; even the desire of escaping them; they
love their servitude."[11]

---

9. Eric Hoffer, The Ordeal of Change

10. Mastery of Fate

11. Jean-Jacques Rousseau, French philosopher, writer and political theorist

As I have already mentioned, it is best to leave these types of people alone, for the vast majority of them can never be fully awakened from their slumber. Unless of course, by some miracle they've caught a glimpse of awareness and became strong in overcoming their conditions. It is our physical environment that promotes out discipline. But for the most part they are an infrahuman race -an unevolved species- who depend on a virtual reality for their happiness. And if you try in any way to tamper with this 'reality', they will with all certainty, attack you for attempting to destroy the elaborate illusion that was created for them. H.L. Menken wrote:

> "The average man does not want to be free. He simply wants to be safe."

In the movie the Matrix Morpheus tells Neo:

> "The people we are trying to save, are plugged into the very same system we are trying to destroy. They depend on that system for their happiness..."

That 'system' is whatever 'reality' that Monkey is 'plugged' into: sports, drugs, religion, etc. Unfortunately, many in this degree suffer from certain level of insanity. Because no sane person, or at least one who can rationalize and has some degree of intelligence, will passively accept such inferior conditions. "The fact that he accepts or borrows the environment produced by others, proves that he either belongs here, or that he does not know where he belongs."[12] One thing for certain is that he belongs within the First Degree of Monkeyism.

---

12. Mastery of Fate, C.D. Lawson

Chapter 2

The Second-Degree of Monkeyism

(The Manufactured Monkey)

"It is part of human nature to regard as sane those people who share the worldview of the majority of society. Somehow, though, we have managed to divide ourselves into two different, mutually exclusive sanities. The people in each society reinforce each other in madness, believing unsubstantiated ideas that are often contradicted not only by each other but also by whatever objective evidence exist on the subject. Instead of having an ever-adapting civilization-wide consensus reality, we have become a nation of insane people able to see the madness only on the other side."

-Orsen Scott Card/Empire

"People everywhere enjoy believing things that they know are not true. It spares them the ordeal of thinking for themselves and taking responsibility for what they know."

-Brooks Attikson

"All propaganda must be popular and on such an intellectual level that even the most stupid of those towards whom it is directed will understand it. People can be made to perceive paradise as hell, and the other way around, to consider the most wretched sort of life as paradise."

-Adolf Hitler / Mein Kempf

This degree should not be confused with middle class mimicry of "keeping up with the Joneses". Those who are classified as existing within the realm of the Second-Degree of Monkeyism, are those who have barely touched the surface of their consciousness; meaning that they have a diminutive awareness of certain things that has happened, or is happening that affects them physically, mentally, and economically -either directly or indirectly- but lack the will to effect any changes.

These Monkeys, like the ones in the degree below, also have a habit of constantly complaining about everything that is wrong with their condition. And just like those in the degree below them, they also make no attempt in trying to make a difference. In fact, the only difference between those in this degree and the ones in the degree below, is that while those who belong to the First-Degree are completely oblivious to everything except what keeps them entertained, those in this degree only think that they know what is really happening in the world when in reality they don't.

"There is a great difference between knowing and understanding; you can know a lot about something and not really understand it."[1]

These types of people are easily recognized as well. They are the ones who caught a glimpse of awareness -a spark of that surreal moment- and now they suddenly feel as if they are 'enlightened' They probably read a few history books, as well as the Bible and Koran, and have taken certain passages and verses and manipulated it for their own personal gain; usually to try and impress others around them.

---

1. Charles F. Kettering

It is these types of people who I have labeled "Manufactured Monkeys', because they have accepted false or inferior information as their truth, then assume a pretentious role of superiority, believing that they are actually knowledgeable in a particular field or science. Then these same people have the audacity to get upset with you if you choose not to accept, never mind conform to their belief. They want you to think and act like them and when you refuse, they actually become bitter with you.

> "If someone isn't what others want them to be, the others become angry."[2]

Recognizing who falls into this degree is actually simple; listen to how a person speaks and then study the way they interact within a social setting, and you will see that their words constantly contradict their actions. They preach one thing and yet do the complete opposite. This is why it is "better to study men than to study books."[3] If you point this out to them, especially among the so-called 'religious' types, they will try to justify their actions by claiming that they are not 'perfect'. But perfection comes from struggling against all opposition; by retaining inner strength through trial and tribulations. One cannot achieve perfection if one does not even attempt to struggle; thus, one must constantly progress against opposing forces.

Then you have those who are found among the so-called 'nationalist' and 'separatist', who, similar to the Monkeys in the degree below them, have a habit of always blaming someone else for their conditions. People of 'color' are always blaming 'whites'. The poor

---

2. The Alchemist

3. The French General and Emperor Napoleon Bonaparte

'whites' hate people of 'color' for no other reason than having melanin in their skin. Everyone hates the government, and to a degree they might even have valid issues for their hatred. But there comes a time in a person's life when they have to stop pointing fingers in every direction and look within themselves to discover the real architect of their conditions. But when you ask them what they are doing to make a difference, their answer is always the same: "One person cannot make a difference." This is a typical excuse that Monkeys use to justify their behavior; the unwillingness to make a conscious change. History has shown that it has always been one person who has created change.

Then you have those who make futile attempts to change certain conditions by joining Movements, participating in group demonstrations, marches, and giving speeches. But what they fail to understand is that their action, though done with good intent and a false belief that they are making a difference, isn't really creating a serious impact. In fact, this is nothing more than a continuous cycle that never fully comes to an end.

As I write this there is a Movement called "Black Lives Matter", which was formed because of the numerous shootings and killings of unarmed 'black' men (and women) by 'white' officers. Though it's a tragedy that 'white' cops -or police in general- are able to kill unarmed 'black' men and never be penalized for their actions, at the same time, 'blacks' kill more 'blacks' over gang affiliations and drug disputes than all the police shootings put together. But yet, no "Black Lives Matter" movement was ever formed to put a cease to these senseless killings.

All the protesting against police shootings of unarmed 'black' men hasn't changed anything, except create a black separatist movement that pushes the agenda that 'Black Lives' are the only lives that matter. Doesn't all lives matter regardless of race? Why wasn't the Movement called "All Lives Matter?" The fact is that even with millions of dollars spent on body cameras to stop the abuse by police officers, shooting and physical abuse has only increased. Why? It's because the police who are committing these criminal acts, are doing so under the ideology of 'white' supremacy which are sanctioned by the Law. This is why a police officer can shoot an unarmed man 14 times in his back while his hands are in the air. The officer only has to claim that 'he felt threatened and followed his training'. Police Officers, like Correctional Officers, have no individual thought; they are 'trained' how to think and act, and this is why they will never be found guilty of any wrongdoing. And so, the killings continue and so do the marches and protest. A never-ending cycle.

Then you have those -like the students that are protesting against gun violence- and trying to get the government to ban the sale of assault weapons, who don't have the slightest clue that what they are doing actually falls into the government plan of subjugating Americans. The government wants to ban the sale, of not only assault weapons, but all weapons in general. This is the first (or is it the final?) step in their New World Order. The Second Amendment of the Constitution of the United States gives the 'People' the "Right to Bear Arms", and when the government becomes tyrannical and oppressive, then the 'People' have the right to rebel against the government. But how will they be able to do that when they have no weapons?

That is just two example that define those with 'Manufactured Consciousness'. While these people think that they are creating a change for the better, in reality, what they are really doing is making their conditions worst by not understanding the outcome. In a book titled, 'Regards from a Dead Princess'[4] which is based on the historical events during the colonial rule over India, there was a dialogue between two Brits that I found to have a profound truth to it:

---

4. Author Unknown

> "All I can say is, if the masses want to take our place, they
> must do more than make speeches and riot occasionally.
> If they developed qualities needed to gain power and
> retain it, then that power will be theirs by right. It may
> take them a long time, but if they succeed it will prove
> that they are entitled to supremacy, and that we have lost
> qualities that enables us to conquer and rule."

It is only when one truly has an in-depth understanding of human nature and come to grip with the reality that those in power are able to continue ruling because they possess no mercy, compassion and are dealers in human suffering, will they be able to make effective changes. Being self-analytical is hard for most people to do because it forces them to discover the true nature of themselves. So, like everyone else they become so immersed in illusions, that as life passes them by their conditions becomes worse, but yet they continue to do nothing but complain. In fact, except for some of the flowery words that some of the more charismatic speakers use -the ones who utilize people to form useless mass movements- the actions of these Monkeys are not much different than those in the degree below them. These types of people are often referred to as sophomoric; people who think that they possess a vast amount of knowledge when in reality they know absolutely nothing at all.

Merriam-Webster's Collegiate dictionary gives the definition of manufacture as "to invent, to fabricate." Most of those who fall into this degree are those who usually become 'trapped' into a particular ideology, that was invented/fabricated by someone else, and now this ideology has become their 'truth.'

Many of these Monkeys are also stuck in the past, glorifying the achievements of ancient civilizations; claiming that these achievements were done by their 'race', and thus take credit for something that they know absolutely nothing about. How could one have created an advance civilization when they neither possess the desire, will, nor the intellect to change their present conditions?

Some become fanatical in their beliefs whether it's political, religious, or racial. According to them their 'truth' is the only truth, and for the most part they actually believe that the diluted information -or misinformation- that they've acquired makes them more intelligent, more conscious, and more superior than the rest of the masses. And to an extent it does at least to those in the degree below.

Since those in the First-Degree lack awareness, (being zombies they have no conscious thoughts), and are either completely illiterate or have a very limited education, they ignorantly believe that the Second-Degree Monkey possesses a high level of intelligence. But this isn't intelligence. What this Monkey possesses is the ability to read at a certain level, and then mimic what he has read without fully comprehending it. A prime example of the social and psychological behavior of these types of people, I can personally illustrate from my own experience as I evolved from my own primate state.

In the mid-80's' I was part of a quasi-religious organization known as the Five Percenters: The Nation of Gods and Earths.[5] Their ideology is based on the belief that there is no such thing as an omnipresent, omnipotent, and omniscience 'Spook God' who sits up in the heavens directing and influencing the destiny of humanity. And that man, specifically the 'black man' was God, and that the 'white man' was the devil.

---

5. This organization was created by a former member of the Nation of Islam known as Clarence 13X, who became a heroin addict and was eventually killed while committing a robbery in a housing project.

Here, I must explain that I am what is referred to as a 'Puerto Rican',[6] but according to whoever merged all the different ethnic groups into 'color', Puerto Ricans are often categorized as being 'black'. This is actually a misconception because there are many Puerto Ricans who have pale skin with blond hair and blue eyes, and some with red hair and green eyes who are labeled as being 'white'.

The truth is that there is no such thing as a 'black' or 'white' race, any more than there is a nationality called 'Puerto Ricans'. Puerto Rico, the island from which Puerto Ricans originated from, simply means "rich port" which was the name given to the island by the Spaniards, would eventually become our 'nationality'. It is real only because our minds identify with it. These 'colors' we label ourselves with are just another illusion that traps our spiritual essence, in this physical reality. The only race is the Human Race.

The ideology of the Five Percenters was easily accepted among people of 'color', because of the many atrocities committed by Europeans throughout history. We were taught that all 'white' people were 'devils' (which is false), and this kept us racially blinded, and mentally locked in a self-contained ideological prison, not realizing that 'whites' weren't the only perpetrators of such evil.

Evil comes in all form: To the indigenous 'Indians' in pre-Mexico before the arrival of Cortez, the 'devil' came in the guise of the Aztecs who enslaved whole tribes to use as human sacrifices as offerings to their gods. In Rwanda, the 'devil' came in the form of the Hutu ("blacks"), who committed mass rape and genocide against the Tutsi (another tribe of so-called "blacks"), simply because of ethnic differences. The ancient Egyptians looked down upon the Ethiopians and other African nations as being socially and

---

6. Borinquen was the given name to the island of what is now known as Puerto Rico by the Indigenous Arawaks/Taino Indians. This is Puerto Ricans refer to themselves as Boricua.

intellectually inferior. The British massacred thousands of Irish. The Serbian, Croatians and Russian murdered each other. The list goes on. Since the birth of humanity, tribes who possessed military strength always conquered the much weaker ones. Might is Right! But it must be understood that it isn't a whole 'race' or a person's 'color', 'nationality', or tribe that is evil but an individual's mind state that is. And when these individuals attain a certain position of power (as I will show in the Third-Degree), they are able to manipulate others with a certain ideology.

As followers of the Five Percenters, we adopted names such as Justice, Supreme, Powerful, Knowledge, Born, and Wise which was supposed to be our attributes; our names were supposed to reflect our character. We gathered in what we called 'ciphers' (circles) to 'build' (talk) about absolutely nothing of substance. The doctrine we were mimicking was based on the belief that eighty-five percent of the masses are symbolically deaf, dumb, and blind because they were ignorant of their true selves. Ten percent of the world's population are the Power Elite, who control ninety percent of the world's resources. The remaining five percent -who we falsely believed was us- are the poor righteous teachers.

We were the epitome of what a contradiction means. We ran around claiming to be 'gods' and yet we were doing everything un-godlike. We drank, smoked, cursed, and created nothing but chaos within our essential nature. Then we had the audacity to pretend that we were 'higher beings' with our inferior intellect, when the reality was that we were nothing more than Monkeys mimicking a doctrine. We actually thought we were intelligent because we could mimic words that sounded impressive. We thought we were thinking for ourselves when in fact we were really nothing more than victims of mind manipulation. Aldous Huxley wrote:

> "The nature of psychological compulsion is that those who act under constraint remains under the impression that they are acting on their own initiative. The victim of mind manipulation does not know that he is a victim. To him the walls of his prison are invisible, and he believes himself to be free. That he is not free is apparent only to other people. His servitude is strictly objective."[7]

I am not personally attacking this 'religion' (though I no longer agree with its ideology), I am attacking the actions of all practitioners of all so-call 'religious' and social groups who do not practice what they preach. I now understand that the foundation of this doctrine was plagiarized from esoteric teachings of how man, regardless of 'color', is able to reclaim his divinity once he is able to rise above his carnal desires and have mastery over his lower self. As with all teachings you have that which is pure and that which has been debased, and this is why Mystery Schools have always existed; to keep esoteric knowledge hidden from the masses. The Ancients understood that once true knowledge found its way into the hands of the uneducated and profane masses, that it would eventually be diluted from its original meaning.

Of course, we were only parroting/mimicking this doctrine without truly comprehending its profound teachings, which was actually distorted by a much more intelligent Monkey who manipulated it to create racial separatism for his own personal gain.

Though I use the Nation of Gods and Earth to describe the actions of a Second-Degree Monkey, this behavior is typical of many practitioners of all religions and organizations, regardless of what they declare themselves to be. Just because a person defines

---

7. Brave New World Revisited

themselves as being something, this doesn't necessarily mean that they are who or what they claim to be. P.D. Ouspensky writes:

> "A man does not merely think his religion or feels it, he 'lives' his religion as much as he is able to, otherwise it is not a religion but a fantasy or a philosophy. Whether he likes it or not he shows his attitude towards [his] religion by his actions. Therefore, if his actions are opposed to those which are by a given religion [,] he cannot assert that he belongs to that religion".[8]

White Supremacy groups like the Ku Klux Klan and the Skin Heads, obviously do not see anything wrong with lynching a person on Saturday night, and then attending church on Sunday afternoon to profess their love for Jesus Christ. They incite fear and feed of raw hatred, and then have the audacity to proclaim themselves to be 'Christians'.

Fanatical Muslims kill thousands of innocent people in the name of Allah, while the Jews commit the genocidal acts against the Arab people, simply because they -the Jews- believe in a perverted doctrine of them being "God's Chosen People".

Its groups like these that preach their love for 'God' and/or humanity, while their actions prove the opposite. Each of these groups falsely believe that they possess 'the truth', when in reality their 'truth' is nothing more than a Manufactured Consciousness that has been programmed into their psyche; giving them the illusion that their dogma is superior to all others. This is how a Second-Degree Monkey can be distinguished from the rest.

---

8. In Search of the Miraculous

Chapter 3

The Third-Degree Monkey

(The Intelligent Monkey)

"A [person] who wishes to achieve great things must learn to deceive".

-Xenophon, Greek Historian

"If people cannot govern themselves, they must be governed by somebody".

-George Bernard Shaw

"The uncanny powers of a leader manifest themselves not so much in the hold he has on the masses, as in his ability to dominate and almost bewitch a small group of men".

-Erich Hoffer

The Third and last degree of Monkeyism are those who possess a much higher level of intelligence than those within the first two degrees. In fact, this person is intelligent enough to know that he is still a Monkey, in the sense, that he has a natural tendency to conform to the 'norms' of society. But unlike those that exist in the degrees below him, this person is fully aware of what is happening in the world around him. His intelligence and consciousness aren't like the Monkeys who have a Manufactured Consciousness -a false awareness- his consciousness has substance and therefore he sees things as they are not as he wishes them to be.

For the most part this person is very deceptive; a demagogue who is able to manipulate words to influence others for his own personal gain. The writer H.L. Mencken had once defined a demagogue as "one who will preach doctrines he knows to be untrue to men he knows to be idiots". He may portray an image as if he is a very studious person who's knowledgeable in a particular field, and he utilizes this knowledge to beguile those less intelligent than he is. Or he might simply be nothing more than charlatan; a fake, a fraud, a person who purposely manipulates certain effects for a particular reason, usually to make what is said sound more impressive than it really is.

> "The charlatan achieves his great powers by simply opening a possibility for men to believe what they already want to believe".[1]

He is the pimp in the pulpit who preaches a doctrine of a 'god'; the separatist who advocates racial hatred; the politician who talks of

---

1. Grete de Francesco

patriotism. But in truth he does not believe in anything he preaches. He only believes in his ability to mobilize the masses as a herd of sheep, and the omnipotent power that comes with it. His strength comes through the ignorance of others. He knows that "once a doctrine, however irrational, has gained power in a society, millions will believe in it rather than feel ostracized and isolated".[2]

This Monkey, just like those who exist within the first two degrees, have absolutely no desire to come out of the illusionary world that was created for him. Or he chose to create for himself. He wants the same thing other people have; big house, nice cars and fancy clothes. But unlike those in the degrees below him, he doesn't sit around complaining about his conditions; he capitalizes off of it.

He wants wealth and power, and just like those in the degrees below him, he has no real desire in attempting to reach the Stage of Man. He doesn't want to deal with the burden of freedom. The Third-Degree Monkey fully understands what freedom represents: pain and responsibility; more importantly, it brings about a feeling of isolation and loneliness. All the great philosophers taught that the more conscious a man is the more miserable he becomes. Michael Ford states:

> "Consciousness is dangerous because it can destroy the perception of conditions of [the] human belief structure - it can free the psych, but the shock of liberation is sometimes too much to bear."[3]

Just like the Monkeys in the degrees below, this Monkey cannot bear the thought of being alone, but at the same time, he sees himself as

---

2. Unknown

3. Luciferian Witchcraft: The Book of the Serpent

being more superior than the two subspecies. So instead of becoming a follower he puts himself in position of power by becoming a leader; he will accept the burden of being a shepherd that leads the flock. But he also knows that the only real power he possesses over his flock is bound up within their mind. "What luck for rulers that men do not think".[4]

This Monkey has invested time and energy into studying human behavior, and thus understands that the vast majority of humanity will easily give up their will to anyone who is willing to rule over them. And the Third-Degree Monkey will happily do so. He knows that most people are spiritually and psychologically weak, and so he will put it upon himself to be their strength. Most people just want to live a 'happy' life, and if someone is in a position to supply the 'happiness' they demand in whatever form it's peddled in, then the masses will freely and gladly turn their will over to them. Isn't this what the masses has been conditioned to accept? To believe in something outside of their own existence? Isn't this why men create gods? Or make other men into idols so that they can have something to worship? In the movie the Avengers, the god Loki in the Odinist mythology says to the masses:

> "Kneel before me. Is this not your natural state? Is it not the unspoken truth of humanity that you crave subjugation? You were made to be ruled [over]. In the end you will always kneel".

Of course, this mind-state doesn't necessarily apply to all who fall into this degree. There are a few individuals who really do want to help awaken others on their journey to reaching the Stage of Man. These individuals such as Mahatma Gandhi, Dr. Martin

---

4. Adolf Hitler

Luther King, and Nelson Mandela -just to name a few- have metamorphosized into great leaders who have changed the course of history for the betterment of humanity. There was no hypocrisy in their words nor in their actions, but unfortunately nature only produces a few of them at a time.

But for the vast majority of them that do consciously and intellectually reach this degree, they tend to usually turn out to be manipulators whose sole agenda is to keep the masses in a state of ignorance. For the most part they are charismatic demagoguery speakers who are able to excite a crowd. And though they possess the intelligence, they lack the desire to strip themselves of materialism. So instead, the Third-Degree Monkey becomes the perfect illusionist and gives the people exactly what they crave for: Hope in exchange for his leadership.

Adolf Hitler wrote:

"My task is not to make men better, but to make use of their weakness".

Whether their ideology is purely political, religious or racial, these leaders are able to exist as long as his followers maintain their ignorance. His job is to make them "love their servitude".[5] Most people cannot, or just plain refuse, to see the hypocrisy of their leader. But when one does look beyond the facade and begin to question their leader, this 'leader' will suddenly become hostile towards them.

A prime example of this is the Civil Rights leader and Black Nationalist known as Malcolm X. When Malcolm X was faithfully parroting the words of his illustrious leader Elijah Muhammed, he was one of Muhammed's most shining stars. But once the veils

---

5. Adolf Hitler

began to fall from Malcolm's eyes, and his perception was no longer distorted -symbolizing the Stage of Man- Elijah became antagonistic towards him.

I am in no way attacking Elijah Muhammed by trying to assassinate his character. I know how offensive followers become of their 'leaders'. I am merely pointing out a spiritual truth of the evolution of Malcolm X. Malcolm understood that no matter how intelligent he was, that he was still nothing more than a Monkey -in the sense- that he was basically mimicking another man's words. Malcolm stated:

"Every thought I had was Elijah Muhammed's thoughts. Every word spoken was Elijah Muhammed's words. Now every thought I have is my own thoughts; every word is my own".

It wasn't until Malcolm X freed himself from the racial ideology that he was finally able to ascend to the Stage of Man. There are many who are trapped in a racial, political and religious indoctrination, and it's only when their eyes are opened that they will begin to think differently from the masses.

"The dissenter of every human being at those moments of his life when he resigns momentarily from the herd and thinks for himself".[6]

But for every individual who finally awakens and breaks free from the shackles of indoctrination, there are thousands who are willing to wear them, and this is where the Third-Degree Monkey reign supreme.

---

6. Archibald MacLeish

Chapter 4
The Stage of Man

"The individual has always had to struggle to keep from being overwhelmed by the tribe. If you try it, you will be lonely often, and sometimes frightened. But no price is too high to pay for the privilege of owning yourself".

-Friedrich Nietzche/Philologist

"The greatest thing in the world is to know how to be oneself".

-Michel Eyguem De Montaigne

"When you exhibit any significant degree of freedom and self-determination in a group of primates that are not self-determined, they will ape their own enslaved condition and demonstrate either a predisposition or a frenzied passion not only to reduce your freedom but, more importantly, the means and methods by which you attained freedom. People are slaves primarily as a result of their own ideas, that in turn starts upsetting the mental mechanism (which can be quite complex) of their enslaved condition."

-Peter Moon Synchronicity and the Seven Seal

Now we come to the Stage of Man. It is only after a Monkey goes through the evolutionary process of "shedding his fur and standing upright"[1] that he becomes a Man. Man used in this context refers to not only the duality of sexes -male and female- but it is also symbolic to an individual who has reached a higher level of consciousness. The conversion from Monkey to Man is considered to be one of the loneliest transformations that one can embark on. According to P.D. Ouspensky:

> "Man as we know him is regarded not as the highest possible expression of his kind, and not as a completed being, but a being in a certain definite phase of his possible transformation. This transformation is considered to be possible in one lifetime, that is, it is considered that a man born in one phase can, during one lifetime, pass into another. If we take the example of a butterfly than man approximately is a caterpillar. And the vast majority die as "caterpillars". But one out of the masses of "caterpillars" There is a small percentage of transforming beings [who are] constantly emerging. These evolving beings are, for us, people of higher minds".[2]

Once an individual has reached this level of awareness, he comes to the realization that his whole existence -his 'reality'- isn't what he has been programmed to believe it is. A part of his psyche has been repressed for so long that now his perception of 'reality' has been shattered; his consciousness slips into a state of shock and his mind becomes crippled.

---

1. To symbolically rise above one's animalistic behavior.

2. Conscience: The Search for Truth

He also comes the profound realization that those with whom he once had something in common with, now no longer share his views. Or more correctly, he no longer shares theirs. Because while his awareness has heightened, creating a shift of perception, those with whom he once associated with are stagnated and still trapped within a manufactured reality. And though it feels good for Man to finally possess his own individual thoughts, (instead of acting upon other peoples' transmitted ideas), this actually creates a confusion among the Monkeys who view things only through a distorted and aggregated pattern.

Man, who himself evolved from a primate state, begins to question the behavior of the masses and their contentment with their enslavement. He sees this as a form of insanity. But since he is the one who is thinking and acting differently than everyone else, it is he who is suspiciously being looked upon as if he's insane. Al Dickens writes:

"If we go along with society's program [we are] considered perfectly normal and healthy people. But as soon as we begin to question the mental establishment, we become misfits as society is concerned."[3]

In truth it is the masses who are insane; they are the ones who are continuously living out their existence doing the same thing on a daily basis and expecting a different outcome. It is said that this is the true definition of insanity. But if Man attempts to free the mind of those he once associated with as he did for himself, he will create a frenzy among them making them antagonistic towards him. They are not looking for freedom or salvation; what they are looking for is security and blissfulness.

---

3. Uncle Yah Yah

"The average [person] does not want to be free. [They] simply want to be safe."[4]

Man, in his genuine attempt in trying to awaken the masses, fails to realize that this puts him in a dangerous position. The Monkeys will become aggressive and might even physically attack him for not sharing their views. Anthony the Great once wrote."

"A time is coming when men will go mad, and when they see someone who is not mad, they will attack him and say, 'You are not mad. You are not one of us'".

So now Man finds himself isolated and completely alone. He begins to understand why many of those who have reached the Third-Degree of Monkeyism have stayed on that level: it's because freedom of mind brings the burden of isolation.

"Freedom, though it has brought [Man] independence and rationality, has made him isolated and thereby anxious and powerless. The isolation is unbearable and the alternative he is confronted with are either to escape from the burden of freedom into a new dependency and submission or advance to full realization of positive freedom which is based upon uniqueness and individuality of [M]an".[5]

---

4. H. L. Mencken

5. Escape From Freedom, Erich Fromm

This is the crossroad for those who have reached this stage: Man either endures what the world sends his way, or he will be crushed. He will either regress back into the conglomerating Monkey mind state, or he will focus his mental energy into becoming a god.

The former happens due to his lack of mental and physical strength. As I have already pointed out, Man has suddenly come to the realization that he no longer shares anything in common with those with whom he once surrounded himself with; they are speaking of things that have no real relevance pertaining to his circumstances. Since he has no one to communicate with and is entirely surrounded by people of inferior intellect, he unconsciously conforms back to his old behavior pattern. The reason this happens is because our minds can only process information that is fed to us through outside experience, so if our experience is superficial -with no form of spiritual or esoteric knowledge- than our reality becomes superficial. This is one of the most essential reasons why a Man of superior intelligence must surround himself with men of like minds. But since Man is constantly surrounded by Monkeys, there is a strong possibility that he will eventually slip back into his former state. The Man in the parable of When The Waters Was Changed illustrated below, is a great allegorical story of how one feels when isolated and alone.

"Once upon a time Khidr, the teacher of Moses, called upon mankind with a warning. At a certain date, he said, all the water in the world which has not been specially hoarded, will disappear. It will be renewed with different water, which would drive men mad. Only one man listened to the meaning of this advice. He collected water and went to a secure place where he stored it, and waited for the water to change its character. On this appointed day the streams stopped running, and the wells went dry, and the man who had listened, seeing this happening, went to his retreat and drank from his preserved water. When he saw from his security, the water again beginning to flow, this man descended among the sons of men. He found that they were thinking and talking in an entirely different way from before, yet they had no memory of what happened, nor of having been warned. When he tried to talk with them, he noticed that they thought he was mad, and showed hostility or compassion; not understanding.

At first, he drank none of the new water, but went back to his concealment to draw on his supplies, every day. Finally, however, he took the decision to drink the new water because he could no longer bear the loneliness of living, behaving, and thinking in a different way from everyone else. He drank the water, and he became like everyone rest. Then he forgot his own store of special water and his fellows began to look upon him as a madman who had miraculously been restored to sanity".
6

The story above is symbolic to how when an individual reaches a higher state of consciousness and his perception changes, he no longer thinks and acts as he once did before. But this makes him different from the group, and since homo sapiens only group together when they share an aggregated 'reality', he no longer has a place with the social setting. He becomes an outcast. Therefore, to alleviate the pain of isolation, Man regresses in order to feel a sense of belonging.

---

6. Tales of the Dervishes, Idries Shah

As Erich Fromm points out:

> "The individual in any given society repress the awareness of those feelings and fantasies which are incompatible with the thought patterns of society. The force affecting the repression is fear of being isolated and becoming an outcast... [Having] thoughts and feelings nobody [else] shares". [7]

Then you have that rare individual who refuses to regress, who will utilize his intellectual energy by mastering his ability to think beyond despair. He learns to manipulate his environment by pure force of will. He becomes the epitome of Nietzsche's Superman concept of an individual who has learned to forgo fleeting pleasures and attain dominance through experience of creative power. Friedrich Nietzsche's Superman concept is based on the belief that the purpose of Man's existence, is to be the type of all-powerful individual.

When Man has reached this stage in his evolution, Nietzsche stresses that isolation is necessary from the masses. With improper cultivating, Man, if not forcefully separated from the masses will eventually ebb back to the level of an infrahuman species.

> "One thing you must set aside in order to fulfill your unique possibility is conformity". [8]

Man must seek perfection in himself. This begins by first stripping himself of all ideologies and dogmas that imprisons him in a

---

7. Escape From Freedom

8. Dennis Kimbro

psychological and spiritual bondage. He disciplines himself in changing his conditions. He buries himself in his task which will eventually produce definite results. Nothing is impossible to a Man who has the desire, determination, dedication, and the discipline to achieve a goal. Upon this road he will find many obstacles in his way, but he must continuously condition his mind in assuming there is a way around them because there usually is. If his mind fails, then he must tap into his inner-self and seek answers from his spirit.

"That which makes the difference between one man and another - between the weak and the powerful, the great and the insignificant is energy, invincible determination, a purpose once formed and then death or victory".[9]

Man has now reached a stage in his evolution where he truly comprehends how magnificent his mind is; that it is both a constructive and destructive force. His mind is both the creator and destroyer of all 'realities'. All that he created -and continues to create- is nothing more than an interconnecting web of divine energy. It is the concentrated energy of his thoughts that give meaning to all experiences, because it is said that thought and energy is the building blocks of all realities. Those who are truly able to comprehend this and acts upon it, are looked upon as being insane. "Because madness is [M]an's desperate attempt to reach transcendence, to rise beyond himself".[10]

Man has learned that the mind is complicated, magnificent, and so powerful that the masses will never be able to fully comprehend it. And because they are not able to do so, fear of Man begins to turn to hatred; isn't it a known fact that people hate what they fear? This becomes dangerous. Man again finds himself at another crossroad:

---

9. Thomas Powell Buxton

He either becomes selected in who he speaks with and thus deals with the ire the rest of the Monkeys will display towards him, or he isolates himself completely and becomes reclusive. Then there's a third option. He becomes a 'Reality Shifter'.

Chapter 5

Reality Shifter

"The logical extension of this practice is... to be all things to all people. When you go into society, leave behind your own ideas and values, and put on a mask that is the most appropriate for the group in which you find yourself".

-Robert Green - 48 Laws of Power

"It is not the strongest who survive nor is it the most intelligent. It is those among us who are the most adaptable to change".

-Unknown

[Survival] requires the ability to play with appearances. To this end you must learn to wear many masks and keep a bag full of deceptive tricks. Deception and masquerade should not be seen as ugly or immoral. All human interaction requires deception on many levels, and in some ways, what separates humans from animals is our ability to be deceived.

-Robert Green - 48 Laws of Power

A 'Reality Shifter' is an individual who is able to fluctuate in and out of different 'realities', without becoming trapped and accepting any of these realities as being the 'truth'. For he understands that 'reality', to describe in the most simplistic term, is nothing more than the belief that objects that we perceive through our five senses is real and have concrete existence outside our minds. But once we step outside the illusionary world that was specifically created for us, we soon come to the realization that 'reality' is nothing more than a false perception of that which has been programmed into our psych. As Morpheus told Neo in the Movie the Matrix:

> "What is real? How do you define 'real?' If we are talking about what you can feel, what you can smell, taste, and see, then real is simply electrical signals interpreted by your brain".

There are individuals who have made it this far who have learned from trial and error -thus firsthand experience- that the vast majority of the human species have a deeply rooted psychological and emotional attachment to these so-called 'realities'. And anyone whose thinking opposes the aggregated groups thinking is often marginalized, and sometimes even physically attacked. Those who are born and raised into a specific ideology, (or even someone whose mind is still impressionable), depend on this ideology to help carry them through life, and doesn't want to be told (nor shown) that their belief is false even if they have a notion of this. Some people rather live a life built on a foundation of lies and be 'happy,' then be face with the truth and be miserable.

In his novel the Traveler, John Twelve Hawks writes about a totalitarian society that puppets a secret group within the government known as Tabula. The word tabula comes from the Latin root word tabula-rasa, which according to Merriam-Webster's dictionary means: "The mind in its hypothetical primary blank or empty state before receiving outside impressions." This group's belief is that it is much easier writing in a 'reality' for an individual when they are young, and thus more impressionable, making them extremely devoted to their doctrine which they will fight and even kill for. The English philosopher John Locke wrote:

"The mind [is] regarded to be blank until it is inscribed upon it. Thus, the mind is built upon received impression plus reflection."

The individual who has reached this stage in their evolution, has finally come to a profound realization that the masses are content with their conditions; this has already been established. To oppose their belief or try to force them to see something other than what they choose to see, only puts the individual in a dangerous position. It is understood that the masses will always be nothing more than a mindless mass of human flesh. If one chooses to use religion, inebriate themselves with liquor, use drugs or get absorbed in the world of entertainment as a form of escapism, then who is Man -who evolved from his own primate state- to try and take away another person's happiness?

But since Man must in some form interact with the masses due to his environment, (unless he becomes a recluse and lives a solitary life), he must learn to deal with them as they are. So, he becomes a Reality Shifter; shifting in and out of multiple realities without accepting, believing, or becoming attached to any of them.

> "The reasonable man adopts himself to the world; the
> unreasonable one persist in trying to adapt the world to
> himself".[1]

Man becomes a chameleon; observing and then assuming the same behavior pattern of each individual he comes across. He masters the art of speaking in the language that they understand. It is a known fact that people tend to feel comfortable dealing with someone who thinks and behaves like them. Your enemy will come looking and sounding just like you. So, this individual must adapt the behavior that will help him assimilate to each person's perception of how they view reality. He learns to maneuver through their imprisonment, because each reality we accept as our truth only confines our thinking within a box.

"It is the intelligence of the inmate who is street wise about his prison, who ducks and plays the game successfully within its rules and confines."[2]

The individual at this stage is only wasting precious energy trying to make people see what they choose not to see. Never has the masses united in order to build a utopian society. It has always been one or two with a higher degree of consciousness, who has tried to awaken other as well. They failed and will continue failing because the masses don't care about freedom; they only care about their immediate gratification.

"The masses never thirsted after the truth. Whoever can supply them with illusions is easily their master; whoever attempts to destroy their illusion is always the victim."[3]

---

1. George Bernard Shaw

2. Children of the Matrix

3. Unknown

Any interaction that Man must have with any Monkeys -regardless of which degree they reside in- must always be within the 'reality' of how they perceive things. It doesn't matter that you know that their belief is based on illusions, what matters is that the person you are dealing with feels comfortable. This isn't deceptiveness but a survival mechanism. As Niccolò Machiavelli wrote:

> "For a long time, I have not said what I believed... and if indeed sometimes I do happen to tell the truth, I hide it among so many lies that it is hard to find."

Chapter 6
The State of God

"There are some men so godlike, so exceptional, that they naturally, by right of their extraordinary gift, transcend all moral judgment or constitutional control. There is no law which embrace men of that caliber. They are themselves law."

-Aristotle

"One should worship a divinity by becoming oneself a divinity. One who has not become a divinity should not worship a divinity. Anyone worshipping a divinity without becoming a divinity will not reap the fruits of that worship."

-Indian Gandharva Tantra

There are many philosophical myths from all cultures and different civilizations about the birth of creation, who and what God is, and how Man came into being. Then there are those who attempt to find a meaningful purpose for their existence here on earth, and for this reason Mystery Schools or Schools of Enlightenment as they are often referred as, were formed. These are the elite institution for the esoteric teachings of cosmology, ceremonial magic, and the development of Man; the divinity of Self.

The State of God in the Egyptian Mystery School was known as Nehast. The word Nehast comes from the Egyptian idiolect meaning "to awaken to a higher existence." What that word refers to is the secret teachings that has opened up the pathway to the different degrees of consciousness, until one has reached a higher state of illumination. They call this illumination god.

Nehast is the balance within our consciousness that allows an individual to discern the intertwining between the physical and the Absolute, because in truth everything within this physical plane is a connection to an abstract reality. As fallen gods, (for we are indeed gods whose consciousness has fallen from a divine state of grace), we've come to perceive the Universe and material matter within this physical plane through a distorted perception.

Institution religion teaches us that God is a benevolent, just, and loving deity who knows no evil. How can this Creative Energy that birthed All things into existence, know no evil? The truth is that the Oneness knows neither good nor evil, for it is a neutral source of emanating intelligent from which all things flow from. It is the primal energy that compromises the life force of all reality. It is amoral; neither good nor bad, unable to be personified; a neutral cosmic energy that permeates all aspects of existence.

In the secret teachings of all the ancient Mystery Schools, neophytes were taught that our minds are a micro reflection of the Microcosm Universe. In essence, our minds are sparks of that Divine Consciousness that defines our divinity. But within time, as we passed through multiple epochs and cycles, we began to lose knowledge of our divine presence; the abstract nature of what we really are, and we started descending into a primitive state of being.

Encumbered in these physical bodies we slowly started losing the identification of our divinity, and thus became trapped within this third dimensional reality; a world of illusion that eventually turned us into nothing more than a mindless mass of human flesh, who are driven by unleashed and uncurbed desires and emotions. We descended from a state of godlike beings to a primitive state of Monkeyism. Now, the Monkey has ascended back into a God.

This was done by awakening what is known as the 'sleeping Serpent'; the energy force that lies in a coil at the base of an individual's spine. As this energy awakens from its dormant state, it travels upward hitting each chakra; the energy points that activates the different levels of consciousness. According to the teachings of Yoga Philosophy, there are seven psychic energy points within the human body. If an individual who possesses an inferior intellect of that of a Subterranean, and suddenly catches a glimpse of awareness; realizing that he can indeed reach a higher state of consciousness by transcending his spirituality, he may do so but only if he chooses to. Choice is what gives homo sapiens the power of free will to create his own destiny. But he must first possess the desire to want to achieve this goal. Once the desire to attain the State of God infects his mind like a disease, he then begins uplifting himself by climbing what I have termed the Seven Steps to Ascension.

The First Step that one must acquire is the impassioned thirst for Knowledge, which is the nourishment and substance that allows an individual's mind to grow. It frees the individual of the mental and spiritual bondage that binds him to an illusional 'reality;' Knowledge strips away all ideologies and dogmas that keeps one imprisoned within a false belief system. J.Z. Knight writes:

> "True knowledge permits us to do away with superficial fears, so that we are no longer enslaved by another's wishes, dogma, or ideologies... knowledge enables us to see heartaches, injustice, and the greed that makes up the greater part of civilization. Knowledge is a reserve, a repository of richness when all else has been taken away from you. Because even if you are imprisoned and stripped of everything, what can never be taken unless of course you allow it- is the knowledge that allows you to create."[1]

The Second Step towards ascension is Understanding. Reading and acquiring new information without truly attaining a firm grasp and apprehensive understanding, is meaningless. People who claim to be 'knowledgeable' because they possess information -but have a minute capacity for understanding- usually don't possess anything of value.

Understanding is the fundamental key, not only of possessing knowledge, but in acquiring wisdom as well. The degree of a person's understanding establishes the capacity of the individual's range of information. Of course, in order for one to attain understanding, especially of a specific subject, one must first have an awareness of that subject, then spend time intensely studying, analyzing and deciphering that subject. All these elements formulate a comprehensive and transcendental state of mind that enables an individual to intuitively recognize truth.

---

1. Ramtha: The White Book

The person who has real understanding of the knowledge that he possesses, and utilizes that knowledge to achieve a greater good, is much more enriched with godlike potentials than someone who merely possesses knowledge but doesn't know what to do with it. Knowledge without understanding is useless! It is said that if knowledge is described as having power, and wisdom is insight; than understanding is symbolic to a protective wear that guards against ignorance.

The Third Step of ascension is Strength. On the path to evolution one must possess mental, physical, spiritual and emotional strength in order to overcome the obstacle one will encounter on that road. The masses, especially those who exist within the First and Second Degrees, are always complaining about their circumstances but unwilling to improve themselves. This, as I have already pointed out, is because they are mentally and spiritually weak. This type of behavior is unfit for a Man; let alone those who are tapping into their godlike potentials. Any person with an excuse about why they can't make things happen their way must be despised.

> "The weak are the most treacherous of us all. They come to the strong and drain them. They are everyone's concern and like vampires they suck our life's blood."[2]

Strength defines the very fabric of who we are in all aspects of our life whether it be mental, spiritual, emotional, or physical. It is the degree of an individual strength that prepares him for the obstacles that he will eventually face. Nature is like a cold-hearted woman who judges individuals by either their strength or weakness. History has proven that those who possess great strength are rewarded, while those who are weak remain in submission.

---

2. Betty Davis

Those who are intellectually and spiritually superior survive in their struggle for existence, because they possess the inner ability to continue striving no matter how difficult the circumstances are. "Everything nourishes what is strong already."[3] Solely to exist is not enough; one must be strong in order to be completely free. This strength must be developed by effort, will-power, and a strong determination. James Allen wrote:

> "You will receive what you earn, no more no less. Whatever your present environment may be, you fall, remain, or rise with your thoughts - your vision, your idea[s]."[4]

The Fourth Step is Discipline. Each individual is who he is and where he is at the precise moment due to his own choosing, regardless of the circumstances he was born into. Nothing in life comes easy, and thus on the road to reaching one's godhead, there will be many obstacles in the way. Strength comes from discipline, but for discipline to be effective one must subject their will to strict regulation; to condition the mind, the body, and the spirit. Those individuals who have transformed themselves from Monkeys to Gods, were able to achieve this through overcoming difficulties that were imposed on them.

This individual must have mastery over his lower self, and the superficial desires that bind him to a material plane. Thus, his discipline is enforced through obedience and order within himself. He must train, mold, and perfect his mental faculties by making his mind vibrate with his spirit. Once he has fully acquired mastery over

---

3. Jane Austin

4. As A Man Thinketh

himself by his discipline, it is then that he begins to evolve into a higher state of being.

The Fifth Step is Perseverance. According to Merriam-Webster's dictionary, perseverance means to "persist in a state of counterinfluence, opposition, or discouragement." It is the determination at all costs to reach the destination or goal that he has set. Once an individual envisions his purpose or goal, he must push himself to the extreme and bring his thoughts and purpose into existence. He must never allow his mind to wander; never allow himself to be distracted from his focal point. It is written that it isn't how many times an individual falls that matters, but how many times he gets up. A rise after a fall generates double strength. Giovanni Casanova wrote:

> "I have always believed that when a man gets it into his head to do something, and when he exclusively occupies himself in that design, he must succeed, whatever the difficulties."

The Sixth Step is Benevolence. Benevolence is the godly act of kindness; a disposition of doing good without expecting anything in return. One of the greatest things an individual can do for his own spirit, is to help those who are truly in need of assistance. This doesn't necessarily mean financially which is much easier to do than giving a part of yourself; your time and your energy.

The act of kindness, of compassion, of giving, and of doing good for others purifies the spirit and the body of all negativities. Only those who possess a godlike nature can truly be benevolent towards others, without expecting something in return. To give or to help others who are less fortunate than you are, is the greatest gift that an individual can bestow upon another.

The Seventh Step is Wisdom. One must never mistake wisdom for knowledge. Knowledge is attained after years of understanding, while wisdom is accumulated learning as well as insight. It is said that a wise person never speaks upon a subject that he or she has no understanding of, because understanding is what makes wisdom powerful.

Wisdom comes when one has reached a certain degree of understanding people, situations -life in general- and have an unusual discernment in dealing with them. A person with wisdom who finds himself in a difficult situation will analyze everything before reacting to the problem at hand.

The individual who has climbed the Seven Steps has in the process unlocked the Mysteries of the Universe, which is to Know Thyself. To know oneself is the foundation of proper cultivating the divinity that lies dormant within us all. He who has reached this state has learned to merge his temporal and spiritual self into perfect harmony. He has stripped himself completely of all illusions. He has become a god.

"There is no entity, nothing, no reality that is greater than you are. For you are the giver of all truth, the creator of all realities, the dispenser of all laws within your kingdom."[5]

---

5. Ramtha: The White Book